# MY SENSES

# Taste

## LET'S READ AV² BY WEIGL™
### ADDED VALUE • AUDIO VISUAL

Go to **www.av2books.com**, and enter this book's unique code.

## BOOK CODE

**B 8 5 7 6 5 9**

**AV² by Weigl** brings you media enhanced books that support active learning.

AV² provides enriched content that supplements and complements this book. Weigl's AV² books strive to create inspired learning and engage young minds in a total learning experience.

# Your AV² Media Enhanced books come alive with...

### Audio
Listen to sections of the book read aloud.

### Video
Watch informative video clips.

### Embedded Weblinks
Gain additional information for research.

### Try This!
Complete activities and hands-on experiments.

### Key Words
Study vocabulary, and complete a matching word activity.

### Quizzes
Test your knowledge.

### Slide Show
View images and captions, and prepare a presentation.

# ... and much, much more!

Published by AV² by Weigl
350 5th Avenue, 59th Floor, New York, NY 10118
Website: www.av2books.com    www.weigl.com

Library of Congress Cataloging-in-Publication Data

Durrie, Karen.
  Taste / Karen Durrie.
     p. cm. -- (My senses)
  ISBN 978-1-61913-312-9 (hard cover : alk. paper) -- ISBN 978-1-61913-317-4 (soft cover : alk. paper)
  1. Taste--Juvenile literature. I. Title.
  QP456.D87 2013
  612.8'7--dc23
                              2012000462

Printed in the United States of America in North Mankato, Minnesota
1 2 3 4 5 6 7 8 9 0  16 15 14 13 12

062012
WEP050412

Project Coordinator: Aaron Carr     Design: Mandy Christiansen

Weigl acknowledges Getty Images, iStock, and Dreamstime as image suppliers for this title.

# Taste

In this book, you will learn

- what taste is

- types of taste

- what taste tells you

and much more!

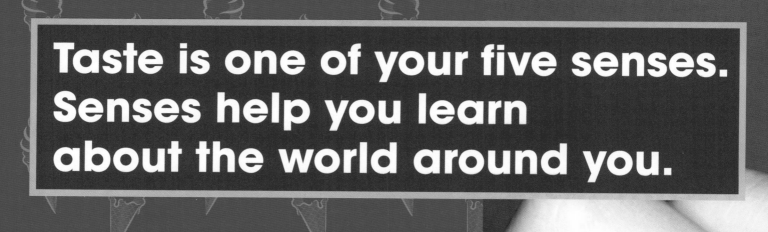

Taste is one of your five senses. Senses help you learn about the world around you.

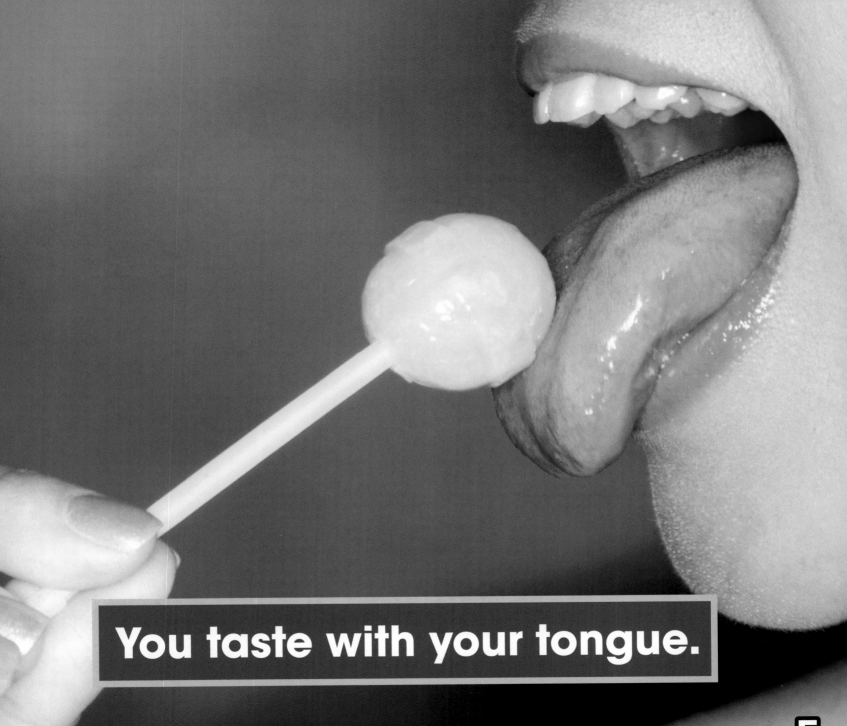

**You taste with your tongue.**

5

**Your tongue has little bumps called taste buds.**

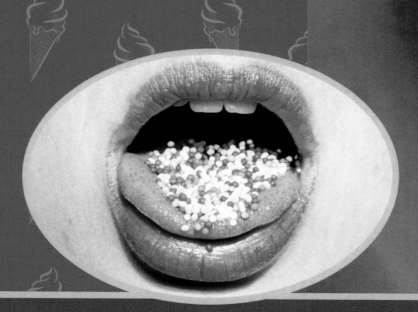

**Taste buds tell you the flavors of food.**

7

# Taste tells you what is salty.

# Popcorn tastes salty.

**Sea water tastes salty.**

**Taste tells you what is sweet.**

**Honey tastes sweet.**

Ice cream tastes sweet.

**Taste tells you what is bitter.**

**Grapefruit may taste bitter.**

**Lettuce may taste bitter.**

**Taste tells you what is sour.**

**Some pickles are sour.**

**Lemons are sour.**

**Taste tells you what is umami.**

**Cheese is umami.**

**Tomatoes are umami.**

**The sense of smell helps you taste food.**

**You smell food when you taste it.**

# What tastes would you find here?

How would these things taste?
Bitter   Salty   Sour   Sweet   Umami

22

# KEY WORDS

Research has shown that as much as 65 percent of all written material published in English is made up of 300 words. These 300 words cannot be taught using pictures or learned by sounding them out. They must be recognized by sight. This book contains 30 common sight words to help young readers improve their reading fluency and comprehension. This book also teaches young readers several important content words, such as proper nouns. These words are paired with pictures to aid in learning and improve understanding.

## Sight Words

| | | | |
|---|---|---|---|
| about | is | tell | would |
| are | it | the | you |
| around | learn | these | your |
| find | little | things | |
| food | may | water | |
| has | of | what | |
| help | one | when | |
| here | sea | with | |
| how | some | world | |

## Content Words

| | |
|---|---|
| bumps | popcorn |
| cheese | senses |
| flavors | taste |
| grapefruit | taste buds |
| honey | tomatoes |
| ice cream | tongue |
| lemons | |
| lettuce | |
| pickles | |

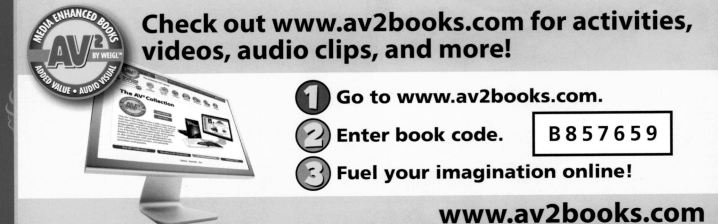

Newbridge Discovery Links®

Exploring CAVES

Barbara Spilman Lawson

Newbridge
A Haights Cross Communications Company

*Exploring Caves*
ISBN: 1-4007-3657-9

Program Author: Dr. Brenda Parkes, Literacy Expert
Content Reviewer: Carol A. Hill, University of New Mexico, Albuquerque

Written by Barbara Spilman Lawson
Design assistance by Kirchoff/Wohlberg, Inc.

Newbridge Educational Publishing
333 East 38th Street, New York, NY 10016
*www.newbridgeonline.com*

Cover Photograph: A cavern in Mexico
Table of Contents Photograph: Gypsum crystal formations in Lechuguilla Cave, New Mexico

Photo Credits
Cover: Sexto Sol/Getty Images; Table of Contents page: Peter Jones; page 4: Dave Bunnell; page 8: Dave
Bunnell; page 9: SuperStock; page 10: Alan Cressler; page 12: Russ Finley/Finley-Holiday Films; pages 12-
13: Peter Jones; page 13: Dave Bunnell; page 14: Bill Lea/Dembinsky Photo Associates; page 15: Chip
Clark; page 16: Charles E. Mohr/Photo Researchers; page 17: Chip Clark; page 18: Chip Clark; page 19:
Chip Clark; page 20: Chip Clark; page 21: NPS Photo; page 22: (left) Annette Summers Engel, (right)
Annette Summers Engel; page 23: David Lazenby/Animals Animals Earth Scenes; page 24: Chip Clark;
page 25: Chip Clark; page 27: (top) Stephen Dalton/Photo Researchers, (bottom) Bob Burch/Bruce
Coleman Inc.; page 29: Courtesy Luray Caverns, VA; page 30: Merlin Tuttle/Photo Researchers

Map on page 5 by International Mapping Associates; diagrams on pages 6–7, 27, by John Hovell

Newbridge Discovery Links®

## Exploring CAVES

Barbara Spilman Lawson

**Newbridge**

A Haights Cross Communications Company

*Exploring Caves*
ISBN: 1-4007-3657-9

Program Author: Dr. Brenda Parkes, Literacy Expert
Content Reviewer: Carol A. Hill, University of New Mexico, Albuquerque

Written by Barbara Spilman Lawson
Design assistance by Kirchoff/Wohlberg, Inc.

Newbridge Educational Publishing
333 East 38th Street, New York, NY 10016
*www.newbridgeonline.com*

Cover Photograph: A cavern in Mexico
Table of Contents Photograph: Gypsum crystal formations in Lechuguilla Cave, New Mexico

Photo Credits
Cover: Sexto Sol/Getty Images; Table of Contents page: Peter Jones; page 4: Dave Bunnell; page 8: Dave
Bunnell; page 9: SuperStock; page 10: Alan Cressler; page 12: Russ Finley/Finley-Holiday Films; pages 12-
13: Peter Jones; page 13: Dave Bunnell; page 14: Bill Lea/Dembinsky Photo Associates; page 15: Chip
Clark; page 16: Charles E. Mohr/Photo Researchers; page 17: Chip Clark; page 18: Chip Clark; page 19:
Chip Clark; page 20: Chip Clark; page 21: NPS Photo; page 22: (left) Annette Summers Engel, (right)
Annette Summers Engel; page 23: David Lazenby/Animals Animals Earth Scenes; page 24: Chip Clark;
page 25: Chip Clark; page 27: (top) Stephen Dalton/Photo Researchers, (bottom) Bob Burch/Bruce
Coleman Inc.; page 29: Courtesy Luray Caverns, VA; page 30: Merlin Tuttle/Photo Researchers

Map on page 5 by International Mapping Associates; diagrams on pages 6-7, 27, by John Hovell

10  9  8  7  6  5  4  3  2  1

LEVEL
**R**